How to Retire Early

The Common Person's Guide

Written by: Blake White

Table of Contents

Chapter Title	Page No.
Prologue	2
The Investor Mindset	4
Replacing Your Budget	16
The Accounts Needed	23
Special Life Events	30
The Growth Years	40
The Retirement Years	51
The Legacy	66
Epilogue	70

Prologue

When you think about your future, what feeling comes up? For most people, it would be anxiety. This is especially true when it comes to one's financials. Your financial future is probably the most important area in your life to plan, but that anxiety will keep you from even thinking about it. This is the reason that I decided I needed to write this book. I speak to people on a daily basis about their finances, and I hear the fear and excuses that keep people from achieving their financial goals. If you can replace those excuses with proper planning and knowledge about the investment world, it will leave you better equipped to achieve your financial goals. The goal I would like to focus on is a goal that I am sure a lot of you have as well, early retirement. Most people think this is a myth or something you have to hit the lottery to do. In reality, it is something that can become very possible with the right combination of dedication and knowledge.

The key is to start with the basics like budgeting and creating the right mindset. Once those are in place you can start gaining knowledge about what investment tools you are willing to use to help achieve your goal. When I say investment tools, I don't only mean stocks and bonds. Those are tools, but I am using the term to even include having the right people around you to help you along. Hopefully, this book will be a solid guide for you to create your own financial empire. One in which everyone is fighting for the same goal, your early retirement.

Chapter 1. The Investor Mindset

The first thing that you will be required to do before even starting the process of reaching this goal is to get into the right mindset. The mind is the number one thing that keeps people from reaching their financial goals. It will constantly come up with excuses for why you can't do something. Just like any other ability, it requires training and discipline to get it to where it needs to be. The main topic I hear that will keep you from where you want to go is risk. The word risk by itself draws up your guard. Probably because you heard some horror story from a family member about a time where they bought a stock and lost all their money. I am not saying that the story isn't true, but all risk is not the same. The key to investing is to take what I would call a "calculated risk". That may sound complicated, but it really isn't. Just be a little smarter with the risk to maximize the return you get for the risk you are willing to absorb. Later on, I will describe the investment products I like to use to create this calculated risk. These are just examples of investments that I feel comfortable using to achieve this goal. You can use my examples and even come up with some of your own.

You should treat your investments like running a business rather than making emotional decisions. You need to work with a financial professional to create the plan that fits you and stick to it regardless of recent market activities. A lot of the horror stories can come from 2008 when the market tanked. People that made emotional decisions that year might have lost around half of their money. If you had not touched anything and stuck to your plan, you probably would have gotten back to where you started within 2 years and now have a hefty profit. Now to answer the people that are sitting there saying to themselves, "I don't want to take any risk." Yes, I understand that in a perfect world we would not have to take any risk with our money in order to achieve our financial goals. Well, unless we go back to the 1980's interest rate environment we won't be able to do that so let's try a way that might actually work. Let us take a second to look at the word risk though. Risk in the investment world seems like a vague description of something scary. In most cases, risk will simply be the amount of fluctuation of the value of the investment.

Let us take a look at one of the riskier investments that we all know about, the stock market. The stock market has many indexes that represent larger groups of stocks that we can look at to get a quick glimpse of how well the market is doing. In this example, I am going to look at three of the most popular indexes: S&P 500, The Dow Jones, and the Russell 2000.

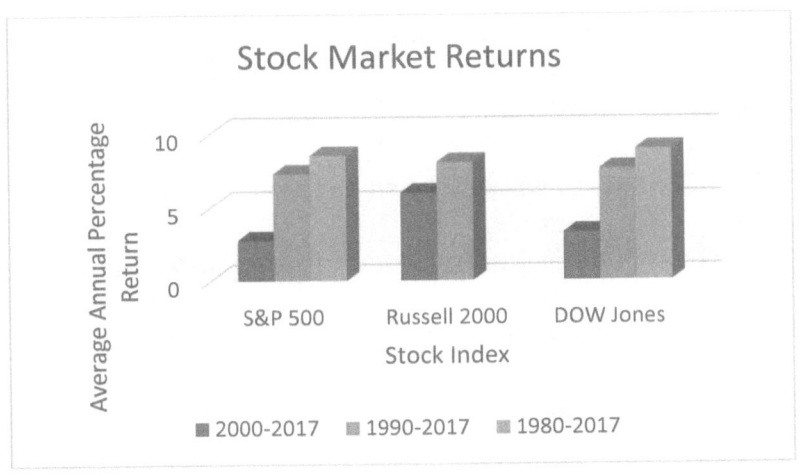

This chart shows that over long periods of time that fluctuations in the market become irrelevant. Out of these three indexes, I think the Russell 2000 is the best indicator of the stock market. However, I included the other two popular indexes so that you can create your own preference. This is why the stock market is a very popular tool to use to save for retirement. Retirement tends to be something that is a long time away when you first think about it. Therefore, the "risk" you take by putting money into the stock market becomes less relevant. I always say the stock market is about playing a game of averages. There are always going to be the bad years that stick in our minds like 2008 or The Great Depression. However, if you take averages of periods longer than a year or two then there are rarely signs of negative returns in the indexes.

Some people have actually been investing for a while. It is important to remember that just because you do something one way does not mean there isn't a better way to do it. At one point, horses were the main type of ground travel. It would seem insane for everyone to ignore the automobile as a way of travel because they have always ridden horses. That same logic goes with investing. Just because you are not familiar with certain investment products does not mean they won't be beneficial to you.

When we look at investing you can simplify it down to two main results you are looking to achieve, growth and income. There are other goals that many would like to achieve, but you should start with just these two for purposes of simplifying. Growth is for the years that you plan to keep working, and income will be for the years after you plan on retiring. The simple formula we are looking for here is to achieve as much growth during the years that you work. Then the total amount of money you have at retirement should be able to produce enough income for you to live off of during retirement years. I know you probably have heard that before on a retirement commercial or by talking with friends but let us look at an even larger goal. What if your investments are able to produce enough income to live off of without touching the principal amount you saved over the years? That is how you build a legacy.

The next question on your mind should be, how much do I need to save. That question has different answers for different people. Some things that can factor into the answer are how many years it is until you are trying to retire and how much do you make. When I think about that question I want to generate enough money to live off the income like I spoke about before. Here is a chart that shows you percentages that you can save in order to produce a number close to that.

Savings Chart

Years Away	Save (Percentage)
35	8%
30	12%
25	18%
20	27%
15	46%

*assumes an 8% return and current income does not change

As you can see in the savings chart, the older you become the harder it will be to reach a goal of early retirement. It is important to remember, that these numbers are just to save for retirement. You will have other financial goals over your lifetime that will need to be added to this percentage. If you get anything from this book, I hope that it is that you need to act now not later. The longer we wait and make excuses why we can't start right now, the further away our retirement gets.

Now most of us are going to need to make some changes in order to find ways to maximize our savings and investments. This includes creating a network of people who will add value to us and reorganizing our budget. Reorganizing the budget is something we will cover in depth during the next chapter but let us take a look at what I mean by creating a network of people. I like to use an analogy with football in it because I like football and I am the one writing the book.

If you are a quarterback standing alone on a field facing eleven members of the defense, you will have a tough time scoring. You need a team that is working together in order to be a productive offense. Since you are the quarterback let us start by drafting a receiver, the financial advisor. This is who you tell which route you want and they catch the ball and make sure it gets into the end zone. Then we need a line to block for us and make sure nothing bad happens to the quarterback, the lawyer. Last, let us get a running back that year after year runs up the middle and gets those extra 2 or 3 yards (or dollars) when we need it, the accountant. These are professionals that most people should at least have a name in mind for when they need one. Financial advisors, accountants, and lawyers fill out the team. I know, I am a financial advisor, of course, I would say they are necessary. Honestly, the reason you need a financial advisor is that they will have access to more types of investments. They will also have experience on how you should invest in order to reach certain goals.

When you choose a financial advisor do not get bogged down when discussing fees. If you are investing with an advisor you will often see a fee of around 1%. This is fairly normal, if they quote you 2% or higher then it is time to look elsewhere. Be upfront with your advisor. Tell them the kind of return you are looking for and when you plan on retiring. They will be able to help pick the proper investments during periods of work and retirement.

An accountant is important because we need to be saving every dollar we can to reach this goal of early retirement. Accountants can often find tax deductions that we are not aware of in order to lower the amount of taxes we pay. A lawyer is probably the least used of the three, but you will want one on standby when you need one. Besides the criminal aspect of needing a lawyer, you might need one to help protect your legacy. Lawyers can help create wills and trusts in order to make sure that your money goes where it should when you are gone. Trust me when I say if everyone saw how many families fight when it comes to inheritance, you would all be calling lawyers right now. Having these three people on your "team", will benefit you in the long run and make sure we are able to score our goal.

Chapter 2. Replacing Your Budget

Once you have figured out how much you need to save, it is time to go find that amount in your budget. I am willing to bet you don't have that much extra laying around each paycheck or you probably wouldn't be reading this book. Which means for those of you that have never created a budget before this is a good time to do one. It is a pretty simple process, just sit down and write every single thing that costs you money each month. Then write the amount each item is costing you, and at the bottom of the page write how much money you make after taxes each month. Also, try to separate each item into one of two categories, necessary and discretionary. Obviously, food and water are necessary whereas cable may be extra. Here is an example of a budget that I have created.

Monthly Budget

Bill	Cost	Necessary or Discretionary
Food	300	Necessary
Gas	200	Necessary
Electricity	150	Necessary
Cable	150	Discretionary
Water	50	Necessary
Car	400	Necessary
Mortgage	1500	Necessary
Golf Membership	200	Discretionary
Total	**2950**	
After-Tax Income	**4000**	

If we look at the total compared to the take-home income of this person, we can see that they can save up to $1050 a month. We should take that number and compare it to the amount we determined earlier that we need to save in order to reach our goal. If we are short at all, then we can look at the discretionary items in our budget to determine what we may cut in order to get closer to the savings amount we need. 401ks, which we will discuss later, tend to make up a good chunk of our savings. Therefore, don't forget to include how much you are saving in your 401k when determining the additional amount that you need to be saving overall.

Other than trimming down to the necessary bills, there are other ways to create savings to help you reach that number you need to hit your goals. One easy to use tool is a credit card. There are a lot of people out there that believe that credit cards are the devil and are only used to keep everyone living in debt. That is only true if you aren't using them the right way. There are a lot of credit card companies that are willing to give you extra benefits like cash back. You can make this type of credit card work for you if you use it the way I am going to tell you. If you set up all of your monthly bills to be charged to your credit card, this will create a discount on your bills each month from your cash back. You just have to be responsible enough to go and pay off each bill as it hits your card. This is just free money and there is no reason not to do it. The cards that have these benefits might require a decent credit score in order to qualify.

If you have already ruined your credit or you don't have credit there are a few things you can do to try and boost it. Some companies are willing to give you a secured credit card in order to build credit. These are just cards that have collateral in case you don't pay it off. You also want to avoid canceling your oldest line of credit and pointless credit checks. It may take some time but it is worth it in the end to receive a card that will give you free cash. There are also apps that will do the same thing these cards will for you. You can do a little research and find which ones you feel comfortable with, but there are many that will give you cash back for purchases such as groceries and clothes.

The biggest advice I can give you for the key to saving is to look for opportunities. There are tons of extra ways for us to make extra cash here and there without a ton of work. I will give you a personal example of an opportunity I uncovered. I have an uncle that was always selling something on the internet. I finally asked him one day where he was getting all of this stuff. He told me that he goes to garage sales every weekend and picks up random things that are undervalued. He then just turns around and sells them on the internet for what they are actually worth. I thought to myself that was too simple and to me if it is that simple then it must be too good to be true. One day though, I got bored enough that I thought I would try it. I am here to tell you that it actually works. You probably won't make enough money to just quit your job but it was a simple and easy way to have some extra income that you can save for your goals. After a while, I actually narrowed my search down to video games because at the time those were the biggest profit makers for me. I was making about $2000 a month just buying and selling video games from people in my area. Now, since then the profits from video games have become smaller and I am searching for my next big profit maker. The point though is that I would never have had that income if I didn't decide to get up on Saturday mornings and look through people's junk. Opportunities are out there and it is just up to us to keep our eyes peeled for them.

Ch. 3 The Accounts Needed

Now we have found the savings within our budget, what is the most efficient way of investing it? The first thing you need to establish is a savings or money market account that will generate some interest for you as well as keep the money available for you. This is going to be your emergency fund and should be priority number one when you are saving. The goal here is to get the emergency fund account to a minimum of 25% of your annual income. We will go over other ways to invest once this account has enough in it later on in this book, so don't get ahead of yourself yet. The interest rate on this account will not be as important as other investments we look at later. However, if you want to achieve every dollar you can you should shop rates. This account could also be used for other reasons. One possibility is opening the account at a local bank or credit union in order to establish a relationship there for future loans. Local financial institutions will often be more lenient with their loans if you have an established relationship with them. Once you decide for yourself which way you would like to use this emergency fund account, it is important to not touch this account unless absolutely necessary. It is mainly to be used to keep you afloat in between jobs or if a large emergency expense happens.

We are all in different situations in life, and there is no one size fits all on how to stockpile your money for retirement. Retirement doesn't mean the same thing to everyone either. Some people see their retirement as finally not having to do anything. Others see retirement as being able to keep working but only when you want to. The best course of action is to get a basic understanding of the different accounts and investments and work with your financial advisor to customize the best plan for you. I have heard from many people that have spoken to advisors before who were uninterested and gave minimum information. If the advisor isn't willing to work with you at the beginning, they don't deserve you when you have built up your fortune. I know that sounds cliché, but I promise you that you will be upset with yourself if you partner with an uninterested professional. Then when you decide to switch to someone else it will cost you transfer fees. It is cheaper to get it right the first time. A good financial advisor will also be able to point you in the direction of other professionals you may need later, which include a lawyer and an accountant. Not everyone is going to need these people right now, but it is important to go ahead and know who you would like to use if the situation does occur where you need them.

Now that the financial advisor can take much of the planning burden from you, let us work on the main account that you can control yourself, the 401k. Most companies offer this as their main retirement benefit now since the death of the pension account. The problem with the 401k account is that most companies don't explain how to correctly set it up or what it should be invested in. It is very common that when setting up the account, you will get to choose from three options: aggressive, moderate, and conservative. The chart below gives a generic guide to go by on what option you should choose.

Risk Tolerance Chart

Risk Tolerance	Years to Retirement	Stock/Bond Ratio
Aggressive	10+	80/20
Moderate	5-10	60/40
Conservative	>5	20/80

Now the next question is how much do we contribute to our 401k? My general rule is the amount they are willing to match. Study your benefits package and determine the maximum amount that your company is willing to do a match contribution for. Mainly, because that is free money and it would be like you giving up a raise not to accept what they are willing to give. It is important to remember that the money in the 401k has not been taxed yet. That means you are actually able to make money off of the government's money until the day comes that you need to withdraw it. Uncle Sam will then ask for his money back. The 401k is the easiest account to save in for most workers especially if the company matches contributions. Let's just say you have a company that matches 4%, and you choose to contribute 4%. That means by you saving 4% of your check, you have taken 8% of the total amount you need to be saving. That is why the 401k is so important, make your company contribute to your future as well. When looking at your company's contributions, make sure you also ask them how long it takes to become vested. Vested means when the company's contributions officially become yours. You will need to make sure you keep an eye on that date, and it may even affect a job change decision. That is because you would essentially be paying them their money back to get out of your job if you were not vested.

Once the 401k is up and running, the rest of the accounts are up to you and your financial advisor. There are quite a few IRA accounts that will provide you with similar benefits. One thing to remember is if you are planning on retiring before age 59 ½ then you will need money invested outside of retirement accounts. Retirement accounts generally receive tax benefits such as money that has not been taxed or a tax deduction. The tradeoff for that benefit is if you make a withdrawal from a retirement account before the age of 59 ½ you will receive a tax penalty of 10%. Knowing that we plan on retiring at age 55, we need to make sure we have enough outside of retirement accounts to provide us with income for those first 5 years. We will discuss this further later when we reach the retirement years discussion.

Chapter 4. Special Life Events

We all know that even if we make the perfect plans for our life that life will somehow turn everything around on us. That is why we need to try and cover ourselves for the situations that are the most common for families. Death can destroy families and end plans to reach our financial goals. That is why life insurance should be a necessary bill for each of us. If you get it earlier in your life it will not even put much of a dent in your possible savings. Like other items we have talked about, it is important to have some knowledge of life insurance so you aren't taken advantage of by an agent. In most cases, term life insurance will be sufficient for what we are looking for. The length of the term should match up to how many years you have left until retirement. That way your family's retirement would not be affected by a premature death. Now there are a lot of things that can go into the amount of life insurance you will need. Most of these categories will be entirely up to your preference whether they are important to you or not.

I like to separate into four categories: debt, income replacement, mortgage, and college education. Take a second to add up all of your loans and credit cards that are out there not including your mortgage. You won't need to include any student loan debt if it was through a federal program because that debt is forgiven at death. If you got your loan through a bank you will still need to include it. Now add your remaining mortgage loan amount to that number. Income replacement is a little trickier than the debt calculation. Since we are going to pay off your debt and mortgage after death lets take those bill amounts off your monthly income. Now let's multiply the remaining income number by how many months you have left until retirement. That will give a solid example of how much income needs to be replaced. The last category is college education and is probably only relevant if you have children. This is also not as straightforward as debt, but there are ways you can figure out this number. If you choose to leave behind funding for your child's college education, then a quick search online may show average tuition rates. Use the current tuition numbers to give you an estimate of how much you need to add to your life insurance. Once you have these four numbers in front of you, add them up, throw in an extra $10,000 to help pay for the funeral and see how much life insurance you need. Most people are surprised by how large this number turns out to be but don't second-guess yourself. That is what you need to take care of your family as well as your family's retirement plan. Just to make sure you fully understand how to do this calculation let me show you an example.

Life Insurance Example

Matt and Jenny have 2 children, a house, a car, and both have jobs. Matt brings home $3000 a month on his paycheck. Jenny also brings home $3000 a month on her paycheck. Their house has $150,000 left on the mortgage loan. Their car has $8000 left on their auto loan. Their car payment and house payment each month adds up to be $1000. Matt is 35 years old and Jenny is 40 years old. They both want to retire at age 55. They also both want to provide for their 2 children's college by putting back $30,000. Let us look at how they should calculate how much life insurance each one needs.

ITEM	MATT			JENNY
Car	$8000			$8000
Mortgage	$150000			$150000
College	$30000			$30000
Funeral	$10000			$10000
Income	$480000			$360000
		$3000		
		-$1000 = $2000		
	(Matt)	X 240 months = $480000		
	(Jenny)	X 180 months = $360000		
Total	$678000			$558000

You can probably get some of this life insurance benefit thru your employer for very cheap. Maxing out the amount they will let you purchase thru work is a good idea. However, keep in mind that if you ever leave that job or decide to switch to being self-employed that the insurance will not go with you. If you think there is the slightest chance of this happening, you should speak with your financial advisor or insurance agent to purchase the amount needed outside of work. To go along with the life insurance conversation is the need for beneficiaries on your accounts. Many people think that a will and testament that is kept in their nightstand is a good estate plan. Some even believe by telling their loved ones who should get each of their assets will take out any issues when they die. Sadly, that is not often the case. It is important to put a beneficiary on any account that you can so that your loved ones can save grief and money from going through the court system for probate.

Going back to where you work, it is also a good idea to go ahead and get disability insurance and long-term care insurance through your employer as well. It is often extremely cheaper to get these through an employer than through at an outside agency. Disability is important because it will provide you with an income stream if you are ever hurt and cannot work for a certain period of time. It is important to remember that short-term disability and long-term disability are two different things and you will need both. Long-term care insurance will provide for you in more serious situations such as when assisted living or nursing homes are required. Most of these situations occur during the retirement years of your life. Unless you want to spend every dollar you and your children have, it may be better to go ahead and purchase some insurance for this. People are often unpleasantly surprised when they find out how much money these situations actually cost.

One major concern for many that have ever been involved in a nursing home situation is how to keep their assets. This is because the nursing home will be able to take assets from them for payment. Proper planning with an estate lawyer can really be a lifesaver in this situation if you plan for it early. One example is to buy 5 years of long-term care insurance. For those of you that are not aware, the look-back period for Medicaid is 5 years. As soon as the long-term care insurance starts, you should transfer the assets out of your name in the most tax-efficient manner. That way when the long-term care insurance expires, you are able to apply and receive Medicaid to pay for the nursing home. That is just one tip for that type of situation, and any estate lawyer would probably be able to tell you which path is going to be the best for you. I just included that tip to let you know how complicated the system can be. However, if you know the system and play by its rules you can make it work for you.

The last life event change I would like to discuss is children. Other than the fact that children force us to reconsider our entire budget, they will include an even more expensive item than all those diapers. That item is education. Most people as parents wish to provide at least something for their kids to go to college. Some people do not and want their kids to have to work their way through college. Although I understand that philosophy, it is much less achievable to do that now than it was in previous generations. That can be attributed to the increased cost of tuition. Tuition costs are more than triple what they were 30 years ago. Whereas, by comparison, the cost of a normal consumer item would only be just over double in that time period. Therefore, the working your way through college philosophy generally ends with a mountain of student loan debt. If we do choose to provide money for our children's college education, it is up to us to again learn what the best way to do that is.

I would say the most popular way I see that done today is through the 529 plan account. This account allows you to save towards college education and not pay taxes on the returns from the investment as long as you use it for qualified educational expenses. That is a definition that is going to change over time, as I am sure laptops weren't thought of as an educational tool in the 1970s. A financial advisor or an extensive internet search should be able to give you the answer to what those are when your children reach college age. Again though, if we decide to do this we need to go back to the budget and edit it to include how much we plan to save towards college each month as a necessary expense.

Chapter 5. The Growth Years

We finally have everything prepared and ready to go, the next question is what we are going to invest in? To recap, we cleaned out our budget to find extra savings opportunities. We created and filled our emergency fund account with 25% of our annual income. We have set up our 401k and contributed to the maximum matching amount. We have added the proper insurances to make sure we are covered if something happens in the middle of our plan. Now let us figure out what kind of investments we need to find to achieve growth.

The years before retirement are what I call the growth years. The return we would like to shoot for is 8%. Unless interest rates are really high you won't be able to achieve that kind of return with CDs or savings accounts. You will have to invest in something with risk involved. Just know that it is unreasonable for you to gain a full understanding of every investment out there. If you did, there would not be much work for your financial advisor to do. The purpose of the descriptions I am going to give you is so that you can have a basic knowledge of these investments when you have your discussion with your advisor about which ones are right for you.

The most common way to reach this kind of return is to work with your financial advisor to build a portfolio of stocks and bonds. An advisor will show you how to properly diversify these investments as well as how to set them up for growth. Stocks are generally invested in for the hopes of the value of the stock going up. This is why it makes it a perfect tool for the growth years. The bonds in the portfolio are more consistent and are usually invested in for the hopes of the interest payments that are paid from it. These will provide some consistency in the portfolio and attempt to keep it from having huge fluctuations. Let us look at an example of investing in stocks and bonds.

Stocks and Bonds Example

Lisa is 35 years old and she meets with an advisor that sets up a portfolio for her of stocks and bonds. Lisa's portfolio is set up to achieve growth because she has 20 years left until her planned retirement. Lisa does not have a 401k so she has to save all of her money herself. Lisa is trying to catch up on her savings because she just started so she is saving $1125 a month of her $50,000 annual salary into this portfolio. The portfolio averages an 8% return a year. This means that Lisa will have just over $617,000 saved up by the time she turns 55.

Stocks and bonds are not our only options though when it comes to what investments can achieve growth. There is a type of investment that is not very well known to the common man called structured products. Structured products are generally more complicated investments and are usually only able to be purchased through financial advisors that have had proper training. What a structured product is able to do in the growth years is transfer some of the risk involved in your portfolio from you if used properly. You are at an advantage especially when it comes to retirement because you know exactly how many years it will be until you need the money.

One type of structured product that is used in the growth years is the market-linked CD. Certain market-linked CDs will allow you to achieve sometimes as much as 2 or 3 times the return of an index by locking in your money with a financial institution. These CDs are usually FDIC insured as well if that makes you sleep better at night. The second type of structured product that can be used for growth is the buffered note. Like the market-linked CD, the buffered note will often allow a 2 to 3 times index return. These won't be FDIC insured like the CD, but they will often provide loss protection up to a certain percentage. These types are products are not appropriate for your entire portfolio, but they are a very useful tool to supplement your stocks and bonds. Let us look at an example of a market-linked CD that is used for growth.

Structured product Example

Erin purchased a 7-year market-linked CD with $10,000 in which the return is based on 200% of an index that the bank created based on certain stocks. Those stocks *achieve a 50% return over the next 7 years. Erin's received a $10,000 profit at the end of the 7 years. That means that Erin received an average of 10.41% return per year which is well over the 8% return we were shooting for.*

All of the previous types of investments we have talked about can be bought in brokerage accounts. Although, your financial advisor is not the only person that can find growth investments for you. Physical assets can also be used for growth. Real estate is the most common physical asset people invest in. However, to use it for growth you will need to work with a real estate agent or gain knowledge of the real estate market yourself. You will need to find undervalued homes or you will need to have abilities to increase the value of homes yourself. I personally would prefer if I wouldn't have to do extra work as I already have a job. If that fits you as well, don't worry there are ways you can include real estate in your portfolio as well. The most common way to do that is to purchase REITs. A REIT stands for a Real Estate Investment Trust. These investments are usually created by a company that is purchasing properties and doing the grunt work while allowing you to participate in some of the rewards if they are successful. A REIT can be a very useful tool, especially because if they are successful they can often achieve the 8% return we are looking for. When buying a REIT, you should look for one that is investing in a category of properties that you think will be successful. I personally like healthcare REITs. That is because the baby boomer generation is getting to the point where they are needing things like assisted living or hospital care. When a generation of that size reaches their golden years, it should create a large need in that industry. This should boost that industry's demand and would be a good opportunity to invest. Let me show you an example of how a REIT may work.

REIT Example

Company XYZ is accepting investments for a non-traded REIT for the next 3 years. They plan on keeping the properties they acquire for 4 more years after that. They will then attempt to sell the properties. They are offering a 4.5% income payment to investors each year and then a portion of the profits from selling the properties at the end. Dave puts $10,000 into this REIT as soon as they begin accepting investments. He receives his $450 each year for the 7 years and at the end, the properties are sold by Company XYZ. The sale of the properties resulted in each investor receiving a 45% return from their original investment. That means that Dave received $14500 at the end of the 7 years. If you add that to the $450 he had already received each year as income, Dave profited $7650 from his original. That is just under 8.5% for his annual return and he was able to achieve the 8% we were looking for.

We discussed before that if we choose to retire early, we need to make sure that some of our investments are not inside retirement accounts. I hope we are choosing to retire early since that is the main concept of this book. It is important to know how much of your savings should go toward this non-retirement account in order to provide for us during the 5-year period before age 59 ½. That number will be different for each person but the following is a general minimum based on your age.

Age 55 Chart

Starting Years until Retirement	Non-Retirement Savings (Percentage)
30	3.6%
20	9.6%
10	33%

You will notice that the numbers are not quite exact to keep the principal intact for those 5 years. It is not as important to have this amount available because it will allow our retirement account to stay in the growth stage for 5 more years. It is ok to overshoot the portion of your savings that should go to the non-retirement account, but it is not acceptable to undershoot it. Saving too much into the non-retirement account will just mean you have more money that has already been taxed. However, saving too little will cause you to receive tax penalties from dipping into the retirement account. Also, these numbers are just a guide to get you to where you need to be and can always be adjusted if you know something about your life that I don't. For example, you might not plan on needing the same type of income when you retire as when you are working. In that case, you can get away with saving slightly less. Although, I would not suggest playing with the numbers this way yourself because your mind will begin to make excuses. Before you know it, you are being forced into a lesser lifestyle rather than being able to choose one.

Chapter 6. The Retirement Years

The one thing that is in a majority of people's hardwiring is the wish to do whatever you want. All throughout our lives, we do what someone else wants. We go to school as a child because our parents want us to get a good education. Then we graduate and get a job doing what someone else wants because we have to pay the bills. Probably 75% of your life you will be doing what other people want. Now some of you might be saying, I started my own business because I don't do what other people want. Well, tell that to your customers. I am sure you would have trouble making any money in a business that didn't do something the customer wanted. That is why retirement is the end goal. The years we finally get to say enough of the treadmill we have been on, I am going to go do something fun.

You might be surprised to know that when I ask people what they want to do when they retire, I rarely am able to get an answer. Even if I do, it is usually something vague like traveling the world or staying at home. Now you might be saying what does this have to do with all those numbers we were working out? The answer is not much, but I think everyone should get a better grasp on what retirement is for them. The system I am giving you will give you the financial freedom to choose what you want to do when you retire, but what good is that if you don't have a plan. I challenge each and every one of you to create an action plan of what your retirement will look like. Maybe we travel for the first few years, and then move closer to the family after that. Maybe we sell the house and move to the beach. The possibilities are endless, but I want to make sure that if we work so hard to get to that point that we make it worth the effort. What we need is called an action plan. An action plan can take a goal that is far off like retirement and break it down into steps that will show you exactly what it will take to get that done. In this case, I would like you to create an action plan for your own retirement. Break it down to what you would like to do each year and an estimate of the costs associated with that. Here is an example of a simple action plan created for retirement.

Action Plan Example

Age	Annual Income Needed	Reason for income	Reason for income	Reason for income
55-60	$100,000	Lifestyle	Travel	Family
60-65	$90,000	Lifestyle	Less Travel	Family
65-70	$90,000	Lifestyle	Less Travel	Family
70+	$80,000	Lifestyle	Family	—

Now to create the numbers for income needed we are also going to have to create a projected budget for retirement. This is where you get to be specific. If your life is going to be exactly how it is now when you retire without the work, then you should already know your budget. Let us say you plan on traveling once a quarter after you retire though.

Then give yourself a budget for travel. Also, some things that you pay for now may not come into play during retirement. For example, you might plan on living in the same house the rest of your life. The house will probably be paid off before you retire which means there is no point in having your mortgage payment on your budget. Use the same template from the monthly budget and create yourself a new tentative retirement budget. Over the years, your desires may change and you can adjust your retirement budget accordingly.

I am off my soapbox now, and we can move on to what I call the retirement years. Well, I guess that isn't a very clever name, but it is the most fitting. There is going to be a very important shift in your investments during this transition period. When you are in the growth years, you are looking for investments that tend to fluctuate more often and get higher returns. We were looking for a minimum of 8% returns during the growth years but with those type of investments, higher returns are possible. Then we make it to the period when we get to the mountaintop and want to turn on the switch we call retirement. These heavy-fluctuating growth investments will need to be converted into lesser-fluctuating income investments. Now, this doesn't mean sell all the investments you have built up over the years and buy CDs. Often, investments can be used for either growth or income. This means you may be able to keep some of your growth investments and just make slight adjustments to them. The return again we are shooting for is 8%. The trickiest part is probably that we have to find investments that will essentially be less risky but not lose our rate of return. As I told you before, risk is the range of fluctuations.

Stocks and bonds are part of these investments that may just require adjustments. Often, stocks will contain what is called a dividend rate. A dividend is simply a company passing out some of it's profits to it stockholders. However, to you, a dividend can be income from a stock. During the growth years, this dividend was probably just set to be automatically reinvested into the stock to help it grow faster. With a slight adjustment, you can make that dividend payment come to you as cash and now you have created an income investment. Bonds are similar but they are generally already used for income. However, a lot of time bond mutual funds are what is found in one's portfolio rather than individual bonds. If this is the case, you will also need to turn the income payment to cash. Let us take a second look at the stocks and bonds example we used from the growth years.

Stocks and bonds example continued

Lisa now has $617,000 saved up and is starting retirement at age 55. Her portfolio continues to earn 8%, but she begins withdrawing her $50,000 a year like she made during her working years. With that average return, her portfolio should be able to provide that $50,000 income until she is close to 100 years old.

Structured products also poke their head into the income investment scenario. Market-linked CDs, that we spoke about earlier can be used as an income investment. Another structured product that will be a useful tool is the structured note. Structured products tend to have hundreds of variations, so there is no point of me trying to describe specifics of a structured note. In general, a structured note will often pay you a set interest rate as long as a market index doesn't go down a certain percentage. These rates tend to be very attractive. Including these products in your portfolio may be required to get the rate of return as high as what we are looking for with our income investments. Now let us continue the structured products example from the growth years.

Structured product Example Continued

Erin has now reached her retirement years and she is no longer looking to lock her money up for periods of time to achieve growth that was achieved by market-linked CDs. She can now convert the portion that was in the market-linked CDs into structured notes. These structured notes provide a straightforward return as long as the index it is based on doesn't have a severe drop.

Physical assets also come back into play when we are looking for income investments. Earlier I told you that real estate can be used for growth. Real estate is also used for income. For example, one can purchase investment homes or apartments and rent these out to tenants. The rent payments will provide a steady income. A lot of people use this tactic, but some overuse it. I will warn you that it will come with extra costs if you don't plan on having to be a landlord as your full-time job. You will need someone to manage all of the properties so that you are not responsible for going to fix the sink at 2 AM. Rental properties can be used as a solid tool for income but beware of the baggage that may come with it.

Tax liens are included in this category as well. Most people have never heard of a tax lien unless you don't pay your taxes or you spend a lot of time at the local courthouse. Tax liens are usually sold by a local government and you can often purchase a property for cheap if you pay the unpaid taxes. Tax liens have many different variations and I recommend that you do plenty of research if you choose to go that route. Like other real estate investments, it can pay off if it works but be a big hassle if it does not. There are many tax liens websites that you can do your own research and determine if they are an investment that you would like to include.

Let us throw a new product into the mix now. I am sure most of you have heard or seen a commercial about this one, annuities. I left annuities out of the growth investment conversation, mostly because the rate of return we need is not reasonable to achieve with an annuity unless interest rates increase. There is one type of annuity, however, that may achieve what we are looking for in both the growth and income areas if planned properly. That annuity is called the variable annuity. The variable annuity has caught a lot of flak over the years. This was caused mainly by greedy advisors that were pushing these investments down people's throats for the high commission rates. If you use a variable annuity for the right reasons, however, it can be an amazing tool for retirement.

The main purpose of a variable annuity is to provide you with guaranteed income for the rest of your life. Therefore, if you are able to find a variable annuity that is willing to pay you what you need to live each year from your current savings then you are done. You did it and you can relax the rest of your life knowing this income will be there. It is important to remember that annuities are treated very similar to retirement accounts for tax purposes. We should only use them for the income after the age of 59 ½. Let us take a look at an example of how a variable annuity could achieve an income goal for the retirement years.

Variable Annuity Example

Let us say that Mike started a non-IRA variable annuity when he was 25 years old. Company ABC told him they had additional benefits where they could offer a 6% roll-up of your benefit amount. This means that regardless of the investment returns, the guaranteed income amount will increase by 6% each year as long as you do not withdraw any money. They also tell him that if you started taking income at age 60, they will provide a 6% guaranteed income for life at that time. The final benefit that Company ABC is willing to provide is a death benefit that *will allow your beneficiary to receive the higher of your investment returns or what you put in minus withdrawals. Mike starts contributing 12% of his income each year into this account which is $12,000 each year. Mike stops his contributions when he hits 55 because he retires. He then lives off of other savings he has until he hits age 60. At that time, he turns on his income benefit. According to the benefits provided, the base amount the income would be based on should be just over $1.3 million. That means the income should be around $78,000 a year guaranteed for life. That amount doesn't quite meet the number we are looking for in order to replace the entire income we made while we were working. If your situation looks like you may need less income, though, this route can allow you not to have to worry about investment returns during the retirement years. Another benefit to look at is the death benefit that protects your beneficiary from investment* *losses if you were to die prematurely. This product tends to provide more security for those people who aren't comfortable with the unknown of market returns if you use it for the income.*

Your financial advisor will tell you the right combination of investments to provide the income you are looking for. It is important to meet with your advisor regularly to make sure your income is still on track to last as long as you need. This is again why you want to make sure your advisor is someone that you like because you will need to see this person quite often over your lifetime.

Ch.7 The Legacy

So far you have learned about the process to set yourself up to succeed at achieving early retirement and the types of investments that can help you get there. When you become successful at these topics, then the goal is within reach. However, what about the future of your family. We talked about some items we should include such as life insurance and death benefits to make sure our families are taken care of in the case of our premature death. There is one thing missing from this plan though, education. If we do not educate and talk to our families about what we are leaving them the money for then all the work we have done to prepare is for nothing. I often see someone who has just inherited a large sum of money from a loved one after they passed and do not know what to do with it. They usually will end up wasting it on material items rather than continue your plan or set up their own. This is because they do not have any education about what the contingency plan is for that situation.

Most people avoid this because it is an awkward conversation to have and I will agree that it is indeed awkward. That is why the easiest way to do this is to include your loved ones in the conversation from the beginning. If you and your wife are planning to retire but you handle all the finances, bring her to the meetings with your advisor. Let her know that you wish to include her in these meetings so that way she can take over the plan if need be. I have never seen a professional football team go out and play a game with no backup quarterback. They have a backup quarterback that has watched the starter every practice and his job is to step in to make it a seamless transition if he is needed. If the backup was not there then they would have to forfeit the game if their quarterback were to get hurt. That is the same thing that can happen to your goals if you do not keep your loved ones in the loop.

Completing this simple task will allow you to leave a legacy instead of an inheritance. An inheritance is when one receives a lot of money from a loved one. A legacy is when one receives the money and the knowledge to provide for themselves. We all strive to be the best person we can possibly be. Although, at some point in our lives we will leave this earth. At that point, the only thing people will have to judge us is from what we left behind.

There is one statement that runs true for every person and that is that life never goes completely as planned. We can do all this work to properly plan our way to an early retirement, but life might have a few bumps along the way. That is why it is so important to work with your advisor and have a written plan. That way you only have to make slight adjustments as time goes on and life starts to throw obstacles in your way. If you try to set it up and then forget about the plan you will have to start from scratch when something changes along the way. It is also important to always keep trying to learn more about different ways we can create savings and ways we can invest it. Over time different opportunities will present themselves as technology changes. Just keep your eyes and mind open so that way you can recognize these opportunities when they appear.

Epilogue

It is key to understand that everything in your life will not be black and white. The world is made up of mostly grey areas. You may notice that many of the items I included did not get into specifics, and the reason is that there is no way I can possibly know what is going on specifically in your life. However, this should serve as a good guide to come back to in order to keep your life on track. Everyone will need to make slight adjustments depending on what your situation is, but the general concept remains the same. The persons that need to know you are your financial advisor, lawyer, accountant, and insurance agent. These people will be able to nail down the specifics of your life, but only if you are able to communicate with them what you are wanting. The main goals of this book were to give you the knowledge to be able to speak about what you need and get you thinking about what it is you want.

If you have the right team of professionals around you, they should be able to cover the rest.

Disclosure

The examples in this book are meant to be educational only and are not recommendations for you by the author or any of his affiliates. You should meet with your financial advisor to determine what investments are suitable for your needs.

www.ingramcontent.com/pod-product-compliance
Lightning Source LLC
Chambersburg PA
CBHW031541210526
45464CB00003B/1100